BEFORE ORANGE
WAS THE NEW BLACK

THE CAMP HILL STORY

BEFORE ORANGE WAS THE NEW BLACK

THE CAMP HILL STORY

DERRICK GIBSON

*To my daughter, who will always be
the most important person in my life.
I will always love you.
See you when I get home.*

*Also, to all of the prisoners and fellow comrades
at SCI-Camp Hill October 25 and 26, 1989,
and those at SCI-Huntington.
Thank you for the support and inspiration.*

ACKNOWLEDGMENTS

I want to take this opportunity to give the Most-High God thanks and praises for allowing this book to come into fruition. It's been a long time coming with much worry, sweat, dedication, and sacrifice. It is the Most-High who gives us creativity, talents, skills and gifts. I am humbled and grateful for his many blessings.

I also want to thank my sister Trina Gibson who has been my supporter and best friend every step of the way. Love you, Sis. Last and certainly not least, I would like to thank Author Trina Brigham for her hard work, dedication and loyalty throughout this process.

Also, Wydu, Byrd, Big Head Beyah, Bro. Farakan, Hilly, E-Mitchell, Ronni Sims Jr., Bro. Gregory, Bro. Calvin, Fat Mike and Big Dee, the ones who helped and supported me at SCI-Pittsburgh right after the Camp Hill riot, and all of the convicts and ex-convicts in or out of the system.

Copyright © 2015 Derrick Gibson. All rights reserved.

ISBN: 978-0-9977815-1-9

Before Orange was the New Black (The Camp Hill Story) is a work of non-fiction. These events and incidents, involving real persons and places, occurred before, during and after the SCI-Camp Hill prison riot.

The author is currently housed in the Pennsylvania Department of Corrections and can be contacted at:

> Derrick Gibson #JP-2190
> SCI Retreat
> 660 State Route 11
> Hunlock Creek, PA
> 18621-3136

Or go online at: AuthorDerrickGibson@gmail.com

NOTE FROM THE AUTHOR

I haven't spoken much about my experience in 1989 at SCI-Camp Hill except a few times over the past 26 years and usually once I've been reunited with another prisoner that was there. But after seeing an episode on the travel channel's "Mysteries at the Museum" on the events at the prison on October 25 and 26, 1989, I realized that none of us who were there ever really spoke or wrote about it, and with the growing interest in the new and next generation of prisoners throughout the system, I've been inspired and encouraged to write about it.

Here it is, so take what you will from it even if it's only for entertainment. I also ask that nobody please take offense or get offended by this book, as it is as real as real can get.

At the time this was written, the sole objective was to have these memoirs in print with the limited resources and stationery material I had, in case my property was lost, damaged or destroyed. Corrections can come later—or by you.

1

I GOT ARRESTED AND WAS COMMITTED TO THE Glenn Mills School for boys in August, 1984, after leaving the now long-gone JFK Stadium on the second night of the infamous Michael Jackson and the Jackson 5 tour. I was there on both nights but Michael wasn't—which I probably should have taken as an omen or a bad sign—but there I was leaving out after the rest of the Jackson clan did their thing, even oldest sister Reebie with her performance and song, "Centipede".

Some young white kid had his little gold chain snatched, and was tussling with a group of young blacks when detectives and a plain-clothes officer came swooping in, chasing and beating any and every young black male in sight. I was very large for my age at the time (six feet tall and 220 pounds at age 16), and stuck out in a purple polo shirt and shorts, and navy blue patent leather Adidas sneakers with white stripes and white socks.

An officer came at me out of nowhere and smacked me on the side of the head with a small ballpoint metal paddle/billy club. My head instantly opened up and blood shot out as I was then surrounded and pummeled with fists, billy clubs, flashlights and whatever else, before I fell to the ground. I was then lifted up by numerous officers like a battering ram and slammed head-first repeatedly into the side of a car door.

I screamed out, "I'm a juvenile!" then heard the officers say, "Oh, shit!" They then stopped beating me and called for an ambulance. But by this time, the damage was done—my head was split and needed stitches, my purple Polo outfit was now dark red and my ego and energy from the concert was gone. The only thing left of that night was the Jackson's electrifying performances, of which the last song performed happened to be "Torture", and my navy blue patent leather Adidas sneakers which wiped off perfectly.

My journey through the system had officially just begun. I was charged with robbery and assault on a police officer and taken to a hospital to be stitched up before landing in the Youth Study Center.

My day in family court arrived in about a month. At trial, my public defender's only defense was to say, "Look your honor, my client has on a pair of one hundred dollar sneakers, so he couldn't have snatched a gold chain." So the female judge said, "Yeah, so how did he get those one hundred dollar sneakers?" and found me guilty of the robbery and assaulting the police officer, who beat the shit out of me and showed up in court smiling and being so nice and polite to the judge.

She then committed me to the Glenn Mills Reformatory School for boys. I landed there in October of 1984, received my degree and a certificate in optics and was released in July, 1985. It was an opportunity to come back and earn a football scholarship to a college but the streets were calling, so I eagerly went back there with my trophies in hand.

I lasted on them a whole month before being arrested again at the still tender young age of 17 in August of 1985. This was my first real encounter with and education in the matrix, the school of hard knocks, better known as the penitentiary.

Although I was more than active in the criminal world, it was basically all petty and nonviolent stuff such as scams, gambling, pickpocketing, snatching money bags and sometimes strong arming.

So this night, after returning back from downtown Center City to West Philly, I exited the subway station at 96th and Market St. to walk to my house on 51st and Hazel Ave. I was detained and questioned by both SEPTA and city police, then arrested for allegedly robbing a homeless man with a group of people although no items were taken and nobody but me, who was by myself, was arrested. While in custody in youth care at the Youth Study Center, the same detectives rear-rested me for four armed robberies in that area.

I was then taken to the notorious adult processing headquarters called the Round House at 8th and Race

St., where the judge certified me as an adult and career criminal at the same time. I was then brought back to the Youth Study Center and placed on the security unit and top floor with all my other juvenile buddies certified as an adult: Troy Robinson, Rob Lee, Hus Molo, Chris Louden, Greg, P-Lap, etc. We spent all our time there just like the adults, playing Nintendo, cards and board games, basketball, watching TV (a lot of cartoons) and even baking cakes and cookies in the home economics class. We even received chocolate milk, cakes or cookies as a snack before bed.

My preliminary hearing was held in family court at 1801 Vine Street. Two of those bogus cases were dismissed because the victims refused to even show up. In a third case, the person showed and flatly stated that I definitely was not the alleged perpetrator in the lineup and in court, so that case was also dismissed. But the fourth case was when and where all of the shenanigans came in to play. Before I entered the room for the lineup, I was stopped in the hallway just as the victims and detective appeared. The detective politely pointed to me and said to the victims, "That's him right there." After that, they gladly picked me out of the lineup and pointed me out in the courtroom where I was then held for trial at City Hall.

I was held at the Youth Study Center on the security unit until I turned 18 years old, then taken on exactly my 18th birthday to Holmesburg Prison.

The older cons, especially the ones who had already been upstate, started schooling me on prison life and had me go down to the law clinic. I then learned from an inmate paralegal that it was an illegal tactic the detective used and to let my public defender know this because the case should have been thrown out by dismissal.

When my public defender came to visit me, I explained this fact to him but the public defender's response to me was, "Well, you should have spoken up then because it doesn't matter now if you did it or not, but how much time are you going to get." He then went on to tell me how I was facing 60 years, but he got me a great deal for 4 to 10 years on both cases.

I didn't want to hear any of that deal shit, and took both to trial. Oddly enough, my public defender did not allow me to take the stand, knowing that I was going to mention the lineup incident. Nor did he ever question them on it during the cross examination.

So, of course, I was found guilty of both crimes and sentenced to a total of 2 ½ to 17 years and shipped off to SCI-Graterford in January, 1988. I was processed as inmate number S0228, then classified to SCI-Camp Hill in April, 1988.

Camp Hill prison was where most of the state of Pennsylvania inmates were housed that were of the ages of 15 to 25, especially if your minimum date for parole was within 10 years. I was right at my minimum and my past 2 ½ years were now spent at, both infamous, Holmesburg and Graterford prisons while not even being out of my teenage years.

I can still remember, to this day, first entering and

walking through Graterford's E block, which housed a total of 800 prisoners on that block alone. The cell block was as long front to back as a city block, with its own chow hall behind it.

At chow time, all 800 inmates would come out at once. The first time I walked down this block with about 20 other prisoners being led to the chow hall, I noticed a huge dead rat swinging from a door cell window with a rope around its neck. It had a blindfold around its eyes and front legs tied behind its back with a makeshift roll-up cigarette in the corner of its mouth. I wasn't afraid because I wasn't no rat and would fight or stab, but I didn't know what to think after that.

The old heads at Holmesburg had somewhat schooled me on upstate prisons. They said things like, "Look young buck, always fight back, win, lose or draw," and "Don't be looking in nobody cell because dudes will take offense to that and even kill you for it."

"Why is that?" I asked innocently, not knowing.

"Because there ain't no telling in the pen and there ain't never no telling what's going down in somebody cell. They could be using the bathroom, using, cutting, bagging or selling drugs or wine, fucking an inmate or guard, holding hostages or even killing somebody, and in here sometimes people get killed for just knowing or seeing too much."

Holmesburg Prison, as well as Graterford was definitely jail in its rawest form in the 1980's, so I expected all prisons to be like those. This was not the case as I hit the compound at Camp Hill.

2

As my first day was ending and I was still trying to grasp this Camp Hill thing all of this newness, I was in my bunk and noticed another inmate stop, look in my cell and then leave. Which I didn't say anything, I just took for granted that he made a mistake and came to the wrong cell.

The next day, while standing at the sink which was at the cell bars, I was brushing my teeth and heard the guard call noon count and the same inmate from the night before walked up again to my cell bars mumbling something under his breath, and walked away.

I then snapped, spitting toothpaste and foam out of my mouth like a madman. "Celly, celly, did you see that?!" I asked and stated at the same time.

As he paused from watching the music videos on BET with his 12" black and white television, he asked me "What's wrong, man?" honestly not having a clue as to what I was talking about.

"That little nigga," I said and went on, "He just came by here and stopped and looked at both of us mumbling something under his breath then walked away, and I saw him looking in here last night, too."

My celly just busted out laughing, and even though I knew that he was from Pittsburgh and they weren't as aggressive as Philly dudes, I had still expected him to go into combat mode with me and couldn't figure out what was so damn funny about it.

He finally composed himself when he saw that I was getting upset and ready to tee off on him, and said, "Yo man, chill out. He was only counting."

I said, "That's what prison guards do."

My celly explained, "Yeah, the guard comes by after him and then they check each other's count."

Which I then asked, "What if it don't match?"

My celly said, "Then they'll both recount until they get it right or figure out who's missing."

So I then said, "So that inmate trustee is helping the guard keep us from escaping if we try, and I don't like it, so he better not come back here counting no more."

My celly started laughing again, then said to me, "Man, that's his job, what you going to do?"

"Fuck his ass up!" I said.

My celly just laughed it off again and left it alone and went back to the music videos. Later that day, the same inmate came up and down the tiers passing out the mail and I again got pissed off.

"What kind of shit is this, man? The same nigga is passing out the damn mail, too!" I said to my celly.

"Yo man, you need to chill out because this is how they operate here at Camp Hill," my celly calmly said to me.

"Yeah, if you say so, but this shit really need to change," was my last words that night as I went to bed steaming. But I watched as the trustee came around again that night taking the count.

The next morning, I caught this trusted inmate in the chow hall during breakfast and got right up in his face, venting, "Nigga, if you come by my cell counting me or my celly again, I'm fucking you up, you understand?"

But he couldn't understand where I was coming from and started pleading for me to understand that it was a part of his job and that he didn't want any trouble. I guess he had never been to Holmesburg or Graterford or been given the drill and lessons that I had, which I took for granted that everyone else had, too.

My southwest Philly/west Philly homeboys Linwood, Ant, Lump and Lil Ronnie pulled me aside and said, "Yo man, leave that cat alone because he'll tell on you and have you put down in "Mohawk".

"What's 'Mohawk'?" I asked.

"It's the hole here under D-block with plastic shields on the bars and no air or fans down there. You sweat your ass off in the summertime. It's a sweat box," they schooled me.

Well, I had definitely decided to leave the trustee and his count alone by the time I had entered the block to go back to my cell when I heard the guard bark, "GIBSON, come here!"

As soon as we had reached the office, the sergeant began saying to me, "Ain't you trying to make parole and go home?" Before I could even answer, he continued, "You're already over your minimum and need a full 9 months upstate misconduct-free, so you leave my trustee alone or you won't make it there anytime soon."

That was the last incident involving me and a trustee ever again at Camp Hill, PA. But I still ended up in two good fights, both while working as an a.m. kitchen worker.

The first was with another kitchen worker on the back dock. We got caught and sent back to the block by our kitchen supervisor but were called back for work the very next morning.

The next was with an inmate named Dango from south Philly who kept coming back up to the counter while I was serving cheeseburgers and I kept putting them on his food tray. The kitchen supervisor had already told me that I could take care of whoever I wanted, but after the 4th time, and not knowing this dude, I began to figure out that this dude was trying me. So we went to the back bathroom and knuckled up before getting caught and being let go by the kitchen staff.

Years later and after being bounced around the prison system, me and Dango ended up becoming good friends. But back then, we were just mischievous kids at Camp Hill, and treated as such.

Back then, it would normally take about 2 to 3 weeks for your money to be transferred from one institution to the next in the Pennsylvania DOC (Department of Corrections). Camp Hill would allow you, upon arrival, to go to the commissary and pick up an indigent bag which contained: 1 generic pack of cigarettes. 1 deodorant, 1 bar of bath soap, 1 bottle of shampoo, 1 bottle of lotion, 2 large sized chocolate candy bars and a small bag of popcorn or pretzels.

No other state prison did that, so there were benefits to being a so-called kid inmate in an adult system back then.

Camp Hill also had its own farm and butcher shop where the inmates worked slaughtering meat and pasteurizing the milk, so were allowed as much milk as we wanted. Some guys even kept stray cats from around the Harrisburg area in their cells. We received pure meat for every meal, even most breakfasts had either bacon or sausage.

We would walk around the compound freely, no passes needed. We had a TV and day room, in one, and a telephone room as well. There was a big and a small yard, the small yard being as large as the big yard is in some of today's prisons. There were free weights, basketball courts, a baseball field, and a dirt track. They even played the music from Harrisburg radio stations on the loud speakers in the towers of both yards whenever we were out there. When you heard the music stop, you knew it was yard-in, and the music blasted so loud that you would definitely know it as soon as it stopped.

In spite of harassing and threatening the inmate trustee and having my two fist fight incidents, I still managed to make parole in September, 1988, and almost exactly around the time that I now had 9 months in upstate and 9 months misconduct-free. That was all it took to be paroled back then with an approved home plan and a job or job training program. You could also use a letter of intent from someone or someplace. Of course, I already had a home plan and I used a letter from Impact Services that they sent back to show the parole board they accepted me in their job training program after I had written to them.

But, yet again, the streets were calling me and yet again I answered and obeyed. So by February, 1989 I was right back at SCI-Graterford as a parole violator, waiting to be transferred back to SCI-Camp Hill.

3

1989 WAS A YEAR OF BLACK AWARENESS AND consciousness for the youth, especially inside the prison system. With rap groups like Public Enemy, N.W.A. and KRS-ONE, we were hearing and learning about the Black Panthers, especially Assata Shakur, George Jackson and Angela Davis. There were also the prison incidents at Attica and Soledad prisons and even right here in Pennsylvania with the "old man" Joseph "Joe-Joe" Bowens, where he was accused of killing both the warden and deputy warden at Holmesburg prison, then retaining guns in Graterford, and then taking the guards hostage for days. Everybody would stop what they were doing and race back to their cells to watch BET whenever they showed Public Enemy's videos "Black Steel and Echoes in the Dark" or "Fight the Power" and be energized and hyped afterwards. We kept hearing, "this generation needs to make its mark" stuff, so we felt empowered and felt the need to bring about change, especially in the prison system, which most of us now were encountering.

This was exactly the wrong time for the PA-DOC to usher in all of these new and radical policies.

We first received notice that our single letter number would be replaced by a double-digit letter, so all inmate numbers in existence would have an "A" placed in front of them. My number became AS0228 instead of S0228, as it had been before. Additionally, all numbers in the future would start with "BA", and so forth.

We now could only address staff as CO or Correctional Officer; no more Prison Guard, Guard or Turnkey. All other staff had to be addressed as Mr., Mrs., Ms., Sir or Ma'am. All prisoners were now to be addressed as Inmate, no Convict or Prisoner stuff.

We had to put in a sick call slip in order to be seen, and there was talk about a co-pay fee. All parole violators would be housed on the same block and were not permitted to be employed.

Worst of all, there would be no more Family Day picnics, only a lifer's and a jaycee picnic once a year.

Now, the Family Day picnics were special to all of us because they applied to all inmates in general population, and they would let just about your whole family in to visit you in the yard or somewhere outside the prison cell blocks, and—bring you food! Yes! Mom and Auntie's home cooking! We were even permitted (but on the down-low) conjugal visits with wifey, baby momma, etc. That one there put the icing on the cake and created a powder keg inside the jail that was just waiting to explode, but staff didn't recognize it or even have a clue as to the pure hell that was boiling and about to spill over.

No one felt our pain except Imam Quadir, the good Muslim and black brother. Bro. Quadir volunteered to take on the role for us as an official big brother, mentor, tutor and teacher, all in one. He would hang out in the yard with us, eat in the dining hall with us or you could catch him on the walkway at any given time just about every day. He was the most popular and accessible staff member to the whole inmate population, no matter what faith or race.

Once again, we perceived the notion that only black people could relate to us, and especially as prisoners. We needed to get back home and around our own kind, which was Graterford for the Philly inmates and Western for the ones from Pittsburgh. This is where we thought Camp Hill would transfer us, and where there would be plenty of brothers and sisters just like Quadir. So the rallying cry began through the Philly guys' call of "Let's kick this shit off, so we can hurry up and get to the party," meaning SCI-Graterford.

4

It began as an average fall day on October 25, 1989 as the sun came up and it was bright, clear and warm throughout the day. The word had been spread around the past couple of days throughout the inmates at Camp Hill of the mini riot that had occurred at SCI-Huntingdon. A Muslim brother had been badly beaten on center by the officers there and had refused any medical treatment.

The next day, a group of inmate Muslim brothers went down to the medical department and retaliated by beating the guards on duty down there. They had barricaded the front of the block also, so it took the guards some time to get in. However, once they did, they severely beat and then dragged inmates from the block all the way to the cages in back of the hole, and laid them out there for hours, battered, bloody and bleeding.

Buzz was all around the compound of how we

needed to act next. There was no plan initially in play but after October 25 and 26, 1989 at Camp Hill, the Huntingdon incident and every other prison incident in the state, county and federal systems in Pennsylvania would be called and classified as a mini-riot compared to it. And the total destruction to the prison by inmates would be unprecedented throughout the United States, even to this day, and none of us, the inmates, staff or system was prepared.

The afternoon yard had been called and, as usual, some inmates went out and some stayed in their cells. It was usually the night yard that everybody you knew would go to. Nobody called a gathering or sent word to come out because none of us expected it at that time and right there and then. As usual, I walked the track and jived and talked shit with the West/Southwest Philly squad: Dino, Tokey, Lil Ronnie, McDuffy, Carmen, Anthony Carnish, Rasul, Silk, Fat Mob Dog, Scarboy, my celly, Joker, etc., and listened to the music that was blasting on the loud speaker. I think Scarboy was drunk, as he usually was, from jailhouse juice/wine.

The big yard was called in at the usual time, in between 2:45 and 3:00. As everybody was headed back to the blocks, the guard in the booth by the blocks came out and pulled Scarboy over for some reason and they immediately began to exchange punches. Scarboy was a young kid like myself at the time, about 19 or 20 years old and a little dude with a lot of fight in him, so he was giving it back to this rather large sized officer/prison guard, when all of a sudden big Sergeant Baker, who was about six foot four and weighed all of 300 plus pounds, came rushing in to grab Scarboy. All of the other officers just stood around watching it, just like the inmates. But as soon as Sergeant Baker grabbed Scarboy and he spun out of his shirt, West Philly boys came to his rescue and started drilling Baker, who staggered, shook it off and gave it back. Next, the Southwest Philly squad came to the rescue and started giving it to both officers.

The first officer who had initially started scuffling with Scarboy ran back into the booth and locked it, then got on his walky-talky, screaming for backup. Sergeant Baker was still mixing it up, knocking inmates back with big haymaker punches and still shaking off the well placed ones that caught him. Blood was already streaming down his face and into the big Viking beard he wore. Although originally grey and black, it was now mostly red.

Sergeant Baker fought fiercely as he continued to take punches, staggered then caught his balance and punched back, until he was grabbed from behind and his feet swept from underneath him. The other officers just stood by frozen and watching. I guess they were just hoping with that the crowd that nobody would start pummeling them. Or was it because of the Huntingdon situation?

As soon as Sergeant Baker hit the concrete, feet were now stomping him unmercifully. Extra security came running down the walkway in the form of about 15 or so officers, and maintenance workers who also showed up in prison trucks and a four wheeler. Inmates fled behind the gate separating the main walkway from the blocks, while others ran to the blocks and started opening cell doors and taking the blocks over from the officers, and holding them hostage. Other inmates started running into the gym, chow hall and furniture factory and grabbing anything that they could think of to use as a weapon or disguise.

The officers locked the fence between them and the inmates, then lifted their fallen comrade, Sergeant Baker up and rushed him to the medical department. The officers and maintenance workers stood back and watched as the white shirt came to the fence and pleaded for the inmates to take it in the cells.

The whole general population was out now and everybody started grouping up: Philly was South, Southwest/West, North, Pittsburgh, Harrisburg and the Whites with the Whites. It sort of looked as if it would be a race thing next because there was no whites in the groups of blacks and no blacks in the one group of whites. Even the guards later admitted on the clip from "Mysteries at the Museum" that they were standing around waiting for a race riot between the inmates, but it never happened. That's what caught both inmate and staff off guard: the white inmates were just as hyped and against the system as we were, and were 100 percent supportive and involved now.

Again, the white shirt stepped to the fence with his bull horn and tried to baby talk everybody to go back to their cells and lock in, as the white inmates started yelling back, "Fuck you, we ain't going nowhere."

Then our Muslim inmate Ameen came to the fence with a couple other Muslim brothers and took charge, talking back and forth with the white shirt with the bullhorn. Whatever was being said back and forth between them could not be heard from where I stood, but what Ameen said next was loud and clear:

"You think that we're playing, you think that we are fucking playing?"

Then he turned around to the soldiers and commanded to them, "Go get him, y'all, and bring his ass right here," and the soldiers ran off towards K-block. Everybody just stood still, waiting curiously, as the soldiers then came back out of K-block speed balling the old, evil (some say racist) officer who worked on K-block, looking totally frail and scared out of his mind.

This old, ornery officer would continuously walk around the compound with a chip on his shoulders. He acted like he owned the place, disrespecting inmates verbally and issuing misconducts for any little thing, especially if he knew you were up for parole or on the honor block, where he worked K-block. He would also come out of the block and walk around the small yard while we were out there, looking for trouble. He would make guys go back in, then go back into K-block before they close and lock the gate, which was right there in front of K-block, so you couldn't get around this dude, and he would have something to say to you at some point.

For some reason, only black inmates had trouble out of him and he would definitely make trouble, where and when he couldn't find it.

Inmates started cheering as they saw who they had captured, and he looked as though he had already been slapped around or roughed up a bit. We were all happy that the old screw was finally getting what was coming to him, as he was placed on his knees in front of the gate facing his fellow officers.

One of the inmates who brought him out had a broken broomstick handle in his hand. I was later told that the broomstick handle had been stuck up the old geezer's ass.

Ameen then stepped behind the wicked officer and grabbed a firm grip on the back of his shirt while holding his other hand out toward the soldier, who placed the broken broomstick handle in Ameen's hand. Ameen took a hold of it and shouted to the white shirt with the bullhorn, "Y'all think that we're fucking playing?" Then he started to furiously beat the old officer in the head. As he crashed the stick upside his head he would be in rhythm, with every word that came out of his mouth, with every lick upside the officer's bloody head.   "You…think…that…we're…fucking…playing…with…y'all…"

The white shirt with the bullhorn threw his hands in the air and screamed to Ameen, "Okay, please don't hit him no more," and "Just let us get him and take him to Medical, that's all we ask, sir." Other officers behind him begged and pleaded, too.

"You ain't got to do that sir, he's old enough to be your grandfather. Just let us take him and get him help," the white shirt continued.

Ameen then yelled back, "Y'all want him? Okay, here he goes!" Then he ordered the soldiers, "Throw his ass over the fence."

The white shirt started yelling, "Noooo," as the inmates yelled, "Catch!" And the old officer was tossed in the air over the fence and all of the officers and maintenance workers scrambled to catch the guy, and actually pulled it off, as he landed on top of them and in some of their arms, and they all fell to the ground. They then immediately ran him down the walkway to medical.

The inmates got upset that they had caught him, and started beating and pushing on the fence, then noticed that it was weak and giving some. They began to kick and rock it back and forth as other inmates ran up with crowbars, saws and whatever else to work on it with. Still, the staff stood there and the white shirt kept pleading and trying to get everybody to lock in their cells.

As soon as the gate busted open, every staff member took off down the walkway and into the administration building, and locked it. There was this one maintenance worker who was about 5 feet 8 inches tall, and at least 350 to 400 pounds. He couldn't even walk fast, let alone run, so he tried to walk up the walkway and step to the side as inmates caught up to him, and a few others that didn't make it.

As he stepped to the side, thinking that the traffic would fly past him, he was surrounded and punches rained down on him. He then fell to the concrete and had his watch removed and his pockets emptied as punches and kicks continued to pummel him. He went out cold and flat, face down on the ground. His pants were then pulled down, exposing his big rhinoceros ass, as inmates stood around laughing and thinking of what to do next.

Someone then ran up with a board and started spanking the maintenance dude's big white ass, which then turned red. "Smack! Smack! Smack!" was all you heard in the air, followed by laughter. I think he was out cold because he didn't move, moan or grunt, not one time. Plus, grown men will usually put up some type of fight for their ass and/or dignity, but this wasn't the case.

Sergeant Baker was the only true warrior on that side, so far, and even the rest of the way through the two day riot at SCI-Camp Hill. As for now, the kids were having a ball giving it to the system, while some of the staff in the system ended up getting two balls, literally.

5

Inmates crowded around the commissary as two jumped on a four wheeler and started joyriding around the compound. Another jumped into one of the maintenance trucks and began ramming into the commissary's metal doors. As the doors began to buckle, the crowd began to call the female commissary staff's name out and shouting, "We're coming in there, baby, and we're going to fuck the shit out of you tonight."

Now, I'm not into raping nobody, but I was interested because that white girl had a body. I mean, a little waist, hips, perky breasts, a fat, firm ass and a gap with a camel toe out of this world. Shit, camel toes weren't even in existence back then, but this white woman definitely had one. She was definitely sexy in her jeans and Reebok sneakers, but she had a nasty and evil attitude towards a lot of inmates.

I, personally, never had any problems out of her and would always make it my business when I went to the commissary to get to her window, to lust off of her and say my sweet little nothings to her. She didn't say much back, but never got nasty or disrespectful towards me. My big black self, with a giant kid-n-play box haircut would spend as much money and as much time as possible; the more stuff I ordered, the longer I would be at her window was the science, so I always walked away with a husky bag.

As those doors began to give in, I thought to myself, "Damn, they're about to do her real dirty, so I got to get mines' early." I hope God forgave my thoughts by now because I was young and curious and never had or saw a white woman naked, in person, at that time. But yes! Damnit! I wanted some of that too bad! So I stood by anxiously waiting for those doors to give up the riches inside.

Those doors finally gave in and everybody started rushing in the commissary and cheering, not knowing there was a back door in the commissary that led to the education building, which they had already gone through. As the locked back door was being discovered and the commissary being rushed, the officer in the education building opened the door and the women came flying out with their shoes in their hands towards the front gate, which was opened for them.

Somebody then yelled, "Look y'all, there goes the women! Get them!" and I looked and saw my Caucasian queen and her Reebok sneakers flying across the grass with other women behind her, running towards the front gate. A few inmates took off after them but immediately stopped, or fell to the ground, as gun shots rang out from the tower at the front gate, covering the women and front gate until they all were out and the gate secured again.

The lust for women got lost real soon as nobody checked the school building for leftovers, but headed straight back to the commissary and started looting it. Inmates first started running out with cartons of cigarettes, then when the cigarettes were gone, boxes of Little Debbie snack cakes, then bags of potato chips, corn chips, nachos, etc., then beef jerkies and cookies, to whatever else that was left and not nailed down, and began to share these looted items with other inmates back at the blocks.

A dice game broke out on the side of E-block and guys were making pretend bets with cartons of cigarettes or whatever, because nobody was actually asked to pay up, so there were no winners or losers because at that point, commissary had no value due to the abundance that was floating around the prison.

Back then, every prison had and stocked its own commissary, so it was like the supermarket had just got raided and items were being handed around at will. I never ate so many barbecue chips and beef jerky in all of my life, and probably never will again. But on October 25th of 1989 we were partying hard in preparation for the party we thought we were going to at SCI-Graterford.

As the make-believe dice game went on, I was still standing and watching, and listening to my funny ass celly joking on the dice and making all kinds of weird and unreal bets with commissary items. My entertainment was disrupted when my boy Dino, who was with his side kick Tokey, tapped my shoulder and said, "Come on, man, let's get some of those cans of tuna and onions from down in the kitchen. Scarboy and a few other dudes are at his cell and making tuna fish sandwiches for the whole West/Southwest squad and need some more stuff."

I said, "Okay, I'm in," and turned and started walking towards the kitchen and saw a big line of dudes at the chow hall and asked, "Why are they in line?"

My boy Dino said, "Oh, some of the inmates are serving chow."

I said, "For real?" I couldn't understand why they would take time out for a riot and do this, but I asked, "What are they serving?"

"Macaroni and cheese with peanut butter and jelly," Dino said.

Then Tokey interjected, "They're at the tables and those guys are waiting for them to get up."

I even started thinking, "Who are the table wipers?" But as I entered the chow hall, I saw that they weren't eating or serving dinner but had numerous inmates across the tables having oral and anal sex with them, and the line was of dudes waiting to get some of the action.

Dino and Tokey looked at the expression on my face and busted out in laughter.

I just kept looking and walking straight ahead.

Camp Hill's chow hall was huge and wide before they now split it in half, and I can tell you without really looking around and counting that there was a good 15 to 20 tables with bodies of live inmates across them getting it in, and with some that had dudes all around them.

At one I heard screams, cries and murmurs, and looked and saw the little 98 pound homosexual, who had female looks and I'd only seen in the big yard, being held down across a table and bleeding out of his ass as an inmate was trying to shove his penis into his mouth. The homosexual was begging and pleading for them to stop, he had already done too many, he said, as tears were streaming down his face.

We got to the back of the kitchen and started grabbing cans of tuna fish, jars of mayonnaise and onions and peppers, as well as bread. I then composed myself and said to Dino, "You ain't funny, nigga, they serving pure dee shit, as in ass, nigga."

Dino said, "Yeah, it's a full scale riot, a once in a life time thing, so you got to experience it raw and uncut, man." Then he added, "Plus, you probably wouldn't have helped me and Tokey grab this stuff."

I just grinned and replied, "Yeah, you're right. This riot is definitely raw and uncut but fuck that, I was going to help you with this food because I'm a fat boy." And we all busted out in huge laughter.

We proceeded out of the back of the kitchen with our dinner items for the night and again passed through the dining hall where the sex orgies were taking place, with willing and unwilling inmates. I attempted to keep looking straight ahead, however I moved my head to the right so as not to look in the direction of the grunts and moans that were coming from my left, when I caught a look at a familiar face that was sprawled out on the table with one inmate on each side of him. Each of his legs were being held in place behind him while a third inmate held his arms in place out in front of him, as he was flat down on his belly with a fourth inmate behind him, in between his legs, and pumping hard in and out of his ass with his dick.

"Oh, shit!" I managed to say out loud.

Dino and Tokey looked in the same direction, then back at me with smiles on their faces, as we all figured out that it was the trustee from a year ago. I just smiled back at them and walked out of the chow hall thinking to myself, "Damn! Things have definitely changed here at Camp Hill."

6

As soon as we exited the chow hall we immediately walked right into a storm of wind and dust blowing around in circles and heard the noise of propellers and saw inmates looking upwards, cheering, giving the finger or shouting, "Fight the power!" with raised fists. I myself began to look up, and saw news and military helicopters flying all around the prison in circles.

Dino then shouted to me, "Don't look, because they're filming and taking pictures." And we held our heads down, then ran to F-block, where Scarboy, Cell and most of the Southwest/West Philly squad were eating tuna fish sandwiches and passing around containers filled with juice.

We dropped our items, which the cans of tuna fish were partially opened by us with can openers in the kitchen, and Scarboy along with his celly was sitting on the bed with a big metal pot that was taken from the kitchen earlier. They took cans and dumped them in to what was left in the pot, along with the big jars of mayonnaise, then took knives and began to cut up the onions and green peppers. They mixed it all together with a giant spoon from the kitchen, slapping big gobs of tuna on bread and handing them to us on already torn potato chip (or whatever) bags.

I was enjoying my globs of tuna and listening to the old heads telling all of us to be aware of the helicopters outside, and if we did go out there while there's still daylight to make sure that we hide or cover our faces from them. I couldn't help but keep looking over at Scarboy because something was different about him. I didn't see any cuts, marks abrasions or swelling, but he looked different and strange.

Dino must have noticed me looking because he said to me, "He shaved all of his hair off his face and head so the police won't recognize him, even his eye brows." Then Scarboy looked up at me with a sneaky grin, as Lil Ronnie patted him on the back and I smiled back, nodding my head up and in support of his new look and disguise.

As the talk and laughter went on someone asked, "Yo, where's T.C.?"

Then somebody answered, "He's still over on H-block guarding his faggot, so nobody can get none."

I didn't even know who T.C. was and asked Dino "Who's that?"

He said, "Oh, that's the boy from Southwest that goes with the white boy faggot with the long brown curly hair, like a girl" Dino then added, "I'm starting to think that T.C. believes that he really is a girl, because he treats him just like one and is over there guarding him with his life."

Now I remembered the white boy that looked like a girl and had long curly hair, and the only time I'd see him is once in a while going to and leaving the chow hall in a hurry with some dude guarding him. He was never out in the yard and the only time I'd seen him by himself was on the walkway coming back somewhere in the administration building, which had to be the counselor's office, the medical department or security, where this other dude couldn't go with him. And he was rushing back to the block, then.

Dino said, "T.C. is in love with boy—he's actually over on H-block with a padlock on the faggot's cell door and standing outside with a football helmet on and swinging a baseball bat."

Everybody then erupted into laughter, which then proceeded with somebody saying, "Let's go over there, y'all, I've got to see this." A sheet was then ripped up and pieces passed around, which we all took a piece and covered our faces like bandits, and began walking over to H-block from F. Sure enough, as soon as we entered H-block and T.C. saw us, he immediately jumped to attention, facing towards us and swinging his bat with his football helmet on his head, just like Dino had said.

T.C. then yelled out, "Y'all going to have to kill me about mines." And somebody yelled back, "T.C., man, it's us, cut it out."

Dino walked up to him and said, "T.C., man, give it a break. He's safe." Then he added, "Come on over with us to Scarboy's cell. We got tuna sandwiches, juice, hooch and everything over there, chilling."

T.C. said, "Naw, man, I'm staying right here until this shit is over." Then he asked, "Can you bring me and my wife some sandwiches over? Because I am kind of hungry."

Dino said, "Yeah, man, I got you." And we turned around in silence and walked back out of H-block.

But as soon as we got back outside we began to crack up with laughter and ran back to F-block. Once we got back to Scarboy's cell my celly Joker said, "That's sad, so can we all have a moment of silence for brother T.C.?" And we all busted out again in pure laughter.

Dino then made and took T.C. his sandwiches back over and Tokey carried the juice, as T.C. stayed on post right. That's exactly where he was, the rest of the night until the state troopers came in and secured the blocks, just like he promised.

7

We then decided to all take showers to wash away any evidence that might be on us, blood or any type of bodily fluids. We also figured that once the state troopers came in and took back over the jail, which was inevitable, it would probably be a while before we were allowed to shower again. We also did it to secure each other as one group showered and the other stood on post, because there were no lights downstairs in the basement showers. The prison had turned off all of the power but the water was still running.

The state troopers had already entered the jail and formed a line that secured the front, inside half of the prison, such as the administration building, medical department, counselor's offices, records room, visiting room, security office, etc. Once they did that, some of the guys who lived down in the trailers that worked outside, even lifers and those receiving furloughs or waiting to be paroled, had hidden and disguised the officers in prison browns, which were inmate clothing, and then snuck them out to the line of state troopers.

Some of those inmates had asked those officers to speak to the parole board for them and on their behalf to the administration so they could get their furlough approved. Prison politics at its very best went down.

After our official prison riot shower was taken we all went back to our individual cells to get dressed again for the rest of our prison combat and/or drama, especially since we were well aware that the state troopers were on their way into the compound. Me and my cellmate got dressed as usual, lotioning up, deodorant, greasing and combing our hair and even applying baby powder as well as the fragrant Muslim oil. Clean underwear, socks, t-shirt and *kufis*—I even put on my brand new pair of sneakers and star and crescent chain, as if we were about to go out on visits or something, not back in the middle of a full-fledge prison riot.

Dino and Tokey met me and my celly back at our cell and Dino promptly said to us, "Yo, y'all, they got the black guard that be working this block up in the front cell handcuffed to the barber chair dressed in prison browns, tight ones like the faggots wear. They shaved his head and mustache and are making him eat pure shit and bread sandwiches." Then added, "One dude even got his hat and shirt on, pretending that he's the officer and the guard is the prisoner now."

Tokey said to us, "Come on, y'all, let's go watch."

My celly said, "Yeah." Then added, "Good, because that motherfucker always be lying on dudes when he works out in the visiting room, to get their visits taken from them, then trying to talk to the dudes' women when he send them back to the block, or try to catch her out in the parking lot."

So we all headed to the front of the block to watch and enjoy the show. When we arrived at the cell the black prison guard was handcuffed to the barber's chair, just as Dino said. He looked scared straight and was wearing our prison browns, with his head and facial hair shaved clean.

There were two inmates in the room with him, which one of them had on the officer's shirt and hat and was puffing on one of the officer's big stogy cigars. He was mimicking the black officer's voice and barking out pretend orders to him, which he would then slap the officer in his face. He started asking the officer questions on pretense as well, then slapping him afterward, telling him to answer, "Yes, sir!" Such as "I'm the officer in charge."

Smack!

Say "Yes, sir!"

And the officer would yell out, "Yes, sir!"

"And I'm going to write your ass up anytime I feel like it?"

Smack!

Say "Yes, sir!"

"Yes, sir!"

"But if you call your woman up and let her know

that I want to fuck her the next time she comes up to visit you, I won't write you up no more, right?"

Smack!

Say "Yes, sir!"

"Yes, sir!"

We were all tickled senseless and laughed hard. Dino walked out of the room, laughing and holding his stomach. The inmate/make believe officer took the big cigar out of his mouth and told the officer, "Here, eat this." Then he stuffed the cigar down the officer's mouth. The officer choked, chewed and swallowed it down, flame and all, which I thought was gross.

The inmate then told his fellow inmate that was already in the room with him before we arrived, "Yo, hand me them sandwiches." His comrade reached down behind him and picked up two large sandwiches wrapped in paper towels and handed one of them to him. As soon as the inmate dressed in the officer's shirt and hat opened the tissue up, you could see and smell the shit that was in between the two slices of bread. He held the sandwich out in front of the officer's mouth, which the officer sort of had to lean forward and bite into it.

"Yummy," the inmate said and wiped the shit out of the corner of the officer's mouth with the paper towel that was with the sandwich.

My celly and I were enjoying the show when Dino came back into the cell and said to me, "Yo, man, go next door and look and see what the police is doing."

The cell we were in had the windows painted black

so you couldn't see in or out of it. It had been converted into a barber/storage room and the bed and desk had been removed and replaced by a barber's chair. So I went next door to look out of the window and see what was going on.

The cell was semi-dark, as all of them were, now that the sun had set and the power was out. There was a blanket mostly covering the cell bars and no name tags indicating that somebody lived there, so I walked straight in and then stopped straight in my tracks. One of the white block officers was down on his knees with his hands across the bed frame handcuffed together but folded as if in prayer, and an inmate was behind him pumping dick in and out of his ass.

The officer was quiet and sullen looking as he looked right up at me. The inmate looked up at me also and started pulling his penis out of the guard's ass, while sweating profusely, and moved to the side for me to get some. I shook my head "no" to him, and went and looked out the window at the state troopers on the walkway. I quickly walked back out of the cell as dude went back to pumping in and out of the guard as if it was nothing.

When I got back in the other room, Dino had this mischievous grin on his face. He asked me, "Fats, did you see what the police was doing?" I then understood how he had set me right up for that one.

"Fuck you!" I snapped.

He must have seen the look on my face because he

calmly interjected, "That dude got a life bid, Fats. He's never going home."

"Still!" I snapped again and left it alone. However, that was the first and only time I have ever seen a man get fucked by another man, and it desecrated me to the point that, even now, I still block it out of my mind.

8

Dino's lecture on prison reasoning and rationale abruptly came to an end and we were interrupted by inmates who were now going from cell to cell on the side of the walkway, handing out the big bars of lye soap and padlocks taken from the commissary. Somebody had come up with a bright idea for everybody on that side to start pelting the state troopers with anything hard to back them up and delay them from coming into the general population, securing the blocks. They even had throwers go up onto the roof with boxes of lye soap to toss at the troopers.

The first bar was tossed off the roof and hit a trooper who instantly went down to the ground in agony and was carried off, to the cheers and howls of the inmates. The trooper was faking it though; that was overkill because he was well padded with riot gear.

Others began throwing stuff out of the windows and off the roof until an order was given to the troopers to aim, and they all immediately raised their guns and aimed at targets in the windows and on the roof. The trooper in charge held a bullhorn and began warning that his troopers would shoot us if anybody else threw any more items at them. At that point, the throwing stopped and the windows cleared of bodies. Even the throwers on the roof came back down.

As we all remained on stand-by, singing Public Enemy's songs, "Fight the Power" and "Black Steel and Echoes in the Dark", we found there was a discrepancy in the inmate leadership. Some brothers who were FOI started camping for the inmate minister Bro. Kareem to replace Sunni Ameen. So Ameen stepped aside and let Kareem handle the negotiations with SCI-Camp Hill's administration and the state trooper in charge, as we waited for the outcome and sang like freed slaves.

Bro. Kareem was handed a bullhorn and he went around from block to block, asking all of the inmates to lock in their cells, but pick one representative from each block to go over to the administration building in the morning for a meeting with the Secretary of the Pennsylvania Department of Corrections, David Owens, and the other bigwigs.

What we didn't know was that they were bluffing us and would get nasty and disrespectful, more so than before, to us. And what they didn't know was that, while they were in the negotiation front with Bro. Kareem, others had gone around from block to block, taking the panels off of the doors. Once these panels were off or loosened, you could just reach your hand out of the bars of your cell underneath the panels, and unlock the door yourself. The locking mechanism was on a track above the cell so when you pulled it back with your hand—Booyaow! It popped the door straight open like cracking a safe.

This was our precaution, in case anything went wrong. We also had a volunteer from another block as our representative because nobody on our block (the parole violator block) wanted to be elected.

So we locked in and most of us were already tired from all the havoc of the day and the block was quiet and peaceful, especially for a prison that had, just moments before, had a full-scale riot going on.

Just before I went to sleep I heard Dino, whose cell was across from mine, calling me in a low tone and I got out of my bunk and came up to the bars of my cell. He was shaking his head back and forth at me, indicating, "No". Then I could hear him speaking to me in almost a whisper, "You don't ever volunteer to be a representative or a negotiator in a prison riot, especially when you're only a damn parole violator." Why in the hell would you meet with them people anyway? Because all they're trying to do is find out who the leaders are and blame everything on them."

"Dino, you're just paranoid man, so go to sleep and leave me alone," I responded back.

"Holla at you in the a.m. homie," Dino replied.

"Audi," I said and climbed back in my bunk.

The block was dead silent. So were the guards who

were posted up front with shotguns. I was sound asleep in no time.

"When I run off I'm stomping, but when I come back…"
NWA (Straight out of Compton)

9

Most of us were awakened the next morning by officers who were passing out bag meals which contained boiled eggs, cereal and milk. We still had a store's-worth of food in our cell, so it didn't matter what they fed us. A whole lot of others must have still been full from raiding the kitchen and commissary as there were no complaints about the meal, or lack of it. Most of us, including myself, went right back to sleep.

Lunchtime came around and, once again, we were awakened by the officers passing out bag meals of baloney and cheese sandwiches and announcing for the representative to call out his cell to be let out for the meeting. This was around 11 in the morning, and I wasn't in the mood for any type of sandwich after the shit ones I saw being eaten last night. But I got up and went over to the sink and washed my face and brushed my teeth, before looking into the mirror and combing my kid and play box, out and up.

I watched as our representative was let out of his cell on the top tier, then proceeded to walk down the tier like he was the president or somebody very important. He was carrying a folder underneath his arm, of which I didn't know or understand the purpose. He even had his reading glasses on, like he did every time he would go to the law library. Maybe he thought he was going to litigate the law.

Me and Joker watched out of the window as all of the representatives and Bro. Kareem were escorted down the walkway surrounded by officers and handcuffed in the front. We looked to see who all of the block reps were and, along with others, we called them out to the fellow inmates on our block on the opposite side of the tier who couldn't see and wanted to know. Then we shouted, "Fight the power!" out the window to them until they were gone out of sight. There was dead silence again on the block after that.

My celly went back to sleep just that fast; he must have been exhausted. Nobody was on their cell bars—not even the instigator and trouble maker, Dino. So I just sat on my bunk in silence and began thinking about my family on the outside and how much I missed them, and also how much fun I had yesterday during this riot shit. So I decided to write a quick letter to let them know why I haven't called yesterday or today, and might not be able to for a while.

I don't know why I thought that the letter would ever go out and reach them. I didn't even realize that it might not, or know that it wouldn't even leave E-block, except inside a dumpster.

Moments after finishing my letter and sealing it into an envelope, someone started yelling out to everybody on the block, "They're coming back, y'all, and they don't look too happy, either." I started looking out of my window, along with my celly who had jumped out of his sleep, but still couldn't see them, as they were still heading dow the walkway towards us.

As soon as they appeared in the distance you could tell that they were angry and upset. They shook their heads, "no", letting us know that nothing came out of it, as inmates started screaming obscenities and our theme song, "Fight the Power" out of the windows. The block representatives started motioning their lips and we understood exactly what they were telling us: "We're coming out tonight!"

The officers who surrounded them and were all friendly and smiles earlier while passing out the bag meals and bringing the "reps" out of their cells, now showed clearly that they were angry and hostile too, and just waiting for a wrong move by the prisoners or a command from their white-shirt and commander. So much so, they didn't even recognize the message that was being relayed to us.

There were cheers and hand claps as the block representative came back on the block and walked back down the top tier with his police escort and head down. "Don't worry about it, pick your head up champ," and "Fuck them cops man," was being yelled back to him, letting him know that we understood him, and that he and they still had our full support. It's on!

Once the representative was secured back into his cell there was dead silence in the air, as everybody listened to him bring us up to date on what had occurred.

"They asked us all to bring our identification cards with us before we were let out of our cell, then they escorted us over to the corridor of the administration building and collected the id's", he said. He then added, "They had already taken Bro. Kareem's last night when they handed him the bullhorn."

We were already used to handing over our id cards for everything that was going to be issued: state clothes, games, commissary, even activity utilities like baseball bats and gloves, basketballs, helmets, etc. So I thought to myself that it probably wasn't strange to Bro. Kareem at the time, but I now had a different idea of where this was heading.

The "rep" continued, "We then waited right there for them to come back. The Superintendent came out with his cronies, which we then asked for the Secretary of the DOC and/or the governor. The Superintendent told us that the Secretary called in sick and the governor said that he was tied up on the golf course."

"Oh, yeah," could be heard from the listeners as we all understood the sarcasm of the Super.

The "rep" then went on to give us the play by play, "We then started running off our demands of immunity and family picnic day brought back, jobs for parole violators and so on, but the Super just laughed at us then yelled, "Fuck y'all, y'all ain't getting shit and y'all better hurry up and take it back to y'all cells before we lock your trifling asses up right now."

The representatives and Bro. Kareem then knew and understood the reason for them wanting the identification cards and what was soon to come to them and for them—the state police and new charges.

"No justice, no peace," was the "rep's" last word and the block fell on dead silence once again. October 26, 1989, has to be the most quieted day in SCI-Camp Hill's history.

There was no power in the prison, no talking amongst the prisoners, except maybe in their cell quietly between the both of them, and there wasn't any more movement. The guards didn't make any rounds nor did they pass out any bag meals for dinner. Just an occasional toilet flushing or sink running was all that you heard, until darkness had set in and pure rage came out.

10

Me and Joker both got tired of just lying in our bunks, waiting for the inevitable to happen, again. We started chit chattering between us about how we both came back as parole violators on new drug charges and beat those cases, but now possibly might have new charges placed on us. But we were content with that, especially since West and Southwest Philly kicked it off and, besides, Scarboy was from 49th and Hoopes St., like Joker.

We started jiving each other about whose hood was tougher—South West or West Philly. Then he stopped and said, "Fuck that. You're from West Philly anyway, so I'm bringing you back home as soon as this shit is over and we get back out there."

We then bragged to each other of how we would roll out the red carpet and pick up the tab for each other, both trying to outdo the other.

He even joked about losing all of the hair on the top

of his head and having a "sun roof" at the age of 23 years old now. He said, "Man, I just woke up one day after turning 22, and all my hair was on my pillow. So I looked in the mirror and said, "Oh, shit, I've got to do something about this!" And I drove straight to the barber shop, sat down in the barber's chair and told him to give me a high top and fade. The damn barber started laughing at me, at which I said, "Mother fucker, what's so damn funny? I'm only 22 years old and I want to wear a high top fade, too, like everybody else my age and I'm paying you to fix it, so fix it, dammit!" But the barber said the only way he could fix it was to cut it all off, and I've been wearing a bald head ever since"

I was rolling around in my bunk, tickled to death.

I had met Joker a few months earlier while we both were at Graterford as parole violators and waiting to be transferred back to Camp Hill. A street comrade of his, Al Regan, had been killed and a card had been passed around in the prison for him, which I signed, to be sent to his family as condolences from prisoners.

Little did I or Joker know that this would be the last time we would ever spend together or see one another, or that he would make it out before me, as I was only waiting on a date and he still had to see the parole board for indirect violations. Nor that he'd be dead before I even got there. But, at that moment forever suspended in time, there we were, brothers and fellow comrades bonded together in arms...

"Freedom to get out to the ghetto no sellout,

Six CO's we got and we aughta put their heads out,
But I'll give them a chance because I'm civilized,
As for the rest of the world they can't realize,
A cell is hell, and I'm a rebel so I rebel,
Between bars they got me thinking like an animal…"

Public Enemy
(Black Steel and Echoes in the Dark)

Dedicated to you:
Keith Baskerville
AKA Joker

11

Our bullshit talk was ended by a "click". Then Joker said to me, "You hear that, man?"

We both got quiet and went to the cell bars. We looked around in the dark as the guards in the front of block started shining their flashlights around and down the block.

"Click, click," we thought we heard again, and heard a guard shout, "They're fucking out again!"

We saw prison guards dashing past our window, shotgun and all. Then, "Click, click, click," as I reached up and popped our gate as well.

Prisoners were dashing down the ties in mad rage, chasing after the guards and screaming, "We're out again! No justice, no peace!"

Pure hell raged as we heard shouts of, "Burn it down! Burn it down to the ground this time!" Fires and smoke started going up from everywhere, as we made to the outside of the block and on the compound walkway.

Some of the guards were being captured and beaten, that didn't make it out of the blocks or out of the compound.

Weapons that had been stashed any and everywhere were being retrieved and passed out to everybody: Knives, chains, bats, crow and metal bars, saws, and even blow torches.

The PA DOC either underestimated us or were just totally unprepared for a full-fledged riot because they never searched anything or anywhere that whole day—not even to make sure that we were truly locked in, and now they were about to pay with lives and millions of dollars in damages.

As the fires were being set, fellow prisoners and comrades sang in harmony, "The roof, the roof, the roof is on fire. We don't need no water, just let the motherfucker burn. Burn motherfucker, burn." To honor the MOVE member brothers who were housed in Camp Hills population, and had to watch the Philadelphia police department drop a bomb on the roof of their house on 60th and Sage in West Philly and not allow the fire department to put it out, as their family members and babies burned and no help came, so the roofs of the commissary, kitchen, gym, chapel and furniture factories were set ablaze.

"The roof, the roof, the roof is on fire…"

"No justice, no peace…"

It was then decided to take one of the maintenance trucks and ram it into the fence to create a hole to escape over into nearby Harrisburg. I don't know if those keys to the vehicles and shops were taken again that night or if everybody still had everything from the day before, but I'm willing to bet my bottom dollar on the latter.

I ran down to the big yard behind the others, who followed the truck down past the track and the baseball and football fields, to the back gate that separated us from the railroad tracks and city of Harrisburg. I stopped by the front yard tower as I saw an inmate who I thought picked up something off the ground, and then ran over and unlocked the tower door, but it happened so fast that at that time I couldn't put it together.

There was a female officer in the tower who was standing out on the platform, bent over the railing and looking down as the door was being opened. However, I ran up and caught a hold of the door as it opened and the inmate was partially inside it. He then spun around and yelled to me, "She got a gun, run!" And I took off while the door was again secured and he was inside the tower with her.

Years later I kept hearing the story about the female officer who got raped at the Camp Hill riot and kept the inmates baby. No, she was with that.

The ramming the fence and making it fall down trick didn't work, and neither did the me being lucky and stumbling across a vulnerable and willing female participant trick, so I headed back up the walk way to E-block and met up my boys, Dino and Tokey. We walked back into the block to try and find my celly,

Joker, and some of the other crew, then head over to check on Scarboy and those dudes on F-block. We entered and walked down the cell block and stopped at a cell where some of the crew were posted outside of. You couldn't help but see black Joe and two others in the cell with one of the now captured officers and the officer was crying and saying, "No, please don't, I got AIDS."

Joe stood directly in front of him while the officer was sitting on the bunk. Joe pulled his penis out and said, "Bitch, I ain't trying to hear none of that. You better open your damn mouth." The officer surrendered and opened his mouth and accepted Joe's penis in it, then started sucking it as the other two inmates stood by and waited for their turns.

It was now known to all of the prisoners that any and everything went on this night, and if you didn't participate then don't say nothing. Especially not to any of the Doc. Staff, property, etc., defense. It was truly for keeps this night.

Joe would end up suffering a blood clot in his head and permanent brain damage that he took from a beating at the hands of the officers once the prison was recaptured, so I guess he had his glory at that moment. Plus, he was a warrior and fought the guards hard and fierce while the beating went on.

The word had passed around that the state troopers were back and had formed a line securing the front half of the compound again, and inmates were turning themselves in, in droves. So most of us headed out onto the compound to see what was going on, and as we arrived, a few inmates were running past us and toward the state troopers, carrying what was clearly a body wrapped in a bloody sheet.

"Damn, a body," I said.

"Yeah, the white boy was a rat, so they did him," Dino replied, then added, "It's for keeps this time. You staying?"

"I'm right here," I answered, then said to them, "Let's find Joker."

We then went back into the block and found him there.

"Yo, man, they just carried a body out to the troopers. You in?" I asked him.

"The fuck do it look like, nigga?" was his smartass reply. Then he said to us, "They got a body wrapped in a sheet on the other side of the block, in the side yard."

This was a grassy area between each block back then that separated the blocks. The day room connected them across like a tunnel for the three blocks, E, F, and G on that side, then the other blocks, H, J, and K on the other side of the compound. There was no I block.

I said, "He was a rat boy," talking about the bloody sheet victim.

"The one out there is a prison guard," Joker said.

I then went to look myself, out of curiosity, to see how bad he was stabbed but didn't see any blood. He lay stiff, straight out. He was tied up and wasn't breathing.

The word soon spread that a prison guard was dead,

and cheers went out as others came over to look at the corpse. Volunteers were asked if anybody wanted to turn themselves in and carry the body to the troopers, but nobody took up the offer.

Dino whispered to me, "That's the damn set up! What the hell do anybody look like carrying a dead police anywhere in a riot?" He then said, "The dumb mother fuckers were so scared that they sat the body out here, thinking that one of the helicopters would come down and grab it. But how is a damn helicopter going to land in between the blocks without tearing up the propellers?" Then he added, "Next the plan is going to be to capture the helicopter when it lands, and then fly out of here with it."

I laughed and said, "Dino, you're fucking stupid."

Me, Joker, Tokey and Dino then walked back outside and watched as some inmates were rolling a big ass tank down the walkway. They were going toward a make-shift barricade on the walkway, where piles of chairs, tables, desks, carts and whatever had been stacked up.

"What the hell is that, and what the hell is it for?" I asked out loud.

Somebody else on the walkway explained, "It's a propane tank from the furniture factory. They're going to make a wick and light it up so it can explode when the troopers barge through it. The dude holding the blow torch is posted right there the rest of the way, so he can light it."

I didn't know what a propane tank was back then

but understood that it must have been some type of liquid gas, and even thought that it was a brilliant idea at the time. And as smoke rose from all around more and more and the prison guards and prison rats were being punished left and right, while others were just scared straight and all of a sudden making mad dashes up to the state troopers, live and surrendering, I knew that this Camp Hill shit here was for real, and paused for a moment, to suck in the moment.

I stood there watching as guys from the compound and trailers were turning themselves in. Some of them had their prized possessions with them, like televisions, mostly 12 inch black and white, radios, sneakers, Bibles or Qurans. I didn't see any photo albums, legal or personal mail, or any important documents.

However, their prized possessions were simply knocked out of their hands with night sticks and they were laid down on their faces, secured with plastic ties, and carried to the yard to lay for the rest of the night, to await the others.

After I had enough of watching that scene, I went back to the block. Dino, my good friend, was at the front of the block looking in the day room as I walked up to him.

"What's up?" I asked him.

"They got one of the guards locked in the back room of the office and they're digging through the wall, trying to get him out of there," he said.

So I went into the day room to take a closer look and, dammit, they were actually digging through the wall with different shit! You could see the hole and the guard sitting in the corner of the little room as far away as possible from the hole, which was maybe only three or four feet, and talking on his walky-talky, "Help, help, hurry, mayday, mayday, they're digging through the wall," he said. Then somebody reached in and grabbed him and started pulling him through the hole. He was holding on the walky-talky for dear life, and then announced on it, "Aw, they got me," as it was then snatched out of his hands and the inmates started playing on it and mocking the officer, saying, "Mayday, Mayday," and "Help me, help me," and "Braker one nine, braker one nine."

Whoever was on the other end kept trying to keep contact and converse, saying, "Is anybody there, is anybody there?" and "Who is this, and what is it that you want?" But the only response the received back was, "Mayday, Mayday", "Help me, help me", and "Braker one nine, braker one nine" before the walky-talky was slammed to the floor and bashed with a hammer. And I chuckled, and walked out of the day room.

12

It was now becoming cold and damp inside the blocks as the rain drops were falling lightly outside and everybody was tracking in and out of the blocks constantly. It seemed like everybody was on the go and nobody could stay still. Most of us were young and didn't drink coffee, or even have much to eat or drink that day, because of the feast that we were still licking our chops from the day before.

There was no heat on because the prison had shut it off. Back then, we had steam radiators and the power house was up at the front end of the compound, which was secured by the troopers. So we began to start more open camp fires outside the blocks, burning wood inside the metal trash cans, and standing around them.

Some guys went and got blankets to throw around themselves, or coats. A few even brought out bags of marshmallows from the commissary and hot dogs from the kitchen. When we weren't roasting and singing our

"Fight the Power" or "The Roof is on Fire" songs, were back on the block, watching the troopers at the window in the back of the blocks.

As the night wore on and time seemed like it had slowed down, we remained the last of the almost 2000 prisoners which had now dwindled down to about 200 or less.

The only major plan or weapons we had were the hostages and the propane tank. There was no plan B, C or D. This was it, and we got burned out thinking about what was going to happen and what end this would eventually come down to.

We even thought that we would have the prison for a few days, and hoped for outside pressure to come and bail us out. It had to be on the news all over Pennsylvania now, and the news reporters and family members were right outside the prison.

Deep down inside most of us were still young, and depending on our parents, girlfriends, etc., to be there. False hope was even given to us with the lie that if you went to the small yard and looked out towards the brewery building where the central office building and executives were, you could see family members crowded outside. But when I looked close, they were people in plainclothes and they didn't look anything like my folks —they looked like off duty cops and law enforcers who came to assist the other team.

All of the West/Southwest Philly guys even came together to take inventory an make sure that everybody had enough supplies in their cells to last, things like commissary, cigarettes, and even matches or lighters. Looking back, I don't even know how we could conceive the notion that after all of the tearing down, burning up, raping, robbing, pillaging, beating and killing that went on, that we would go back in our cubby hole cells all sweet and comfy! But, somehow, we really did and we weren't running to those damn state troopers like the rest of those cowards, turning ourselves in. So, "Bring it on pigs, we're right here," was our false mentality, and we were waiting it out.

Part of the reason that the troopers were waiting so long to take back the prison was that they were waiting on daylight so they could see everything and everybody. The other part was that they were out in the big yard with plenty of horses digging ditches for them to shit and piss in, while the rain was making them muddy and sludgy. They were making real damn holes for us to be put in, and we didn't have a clue.

13

Daylight came shining upon us and the adrenaline we had had slowed down and we were pretty much relaxed. Most of the inmates were back in their cells, with a few dudes still posted outside on the lookout. The dude with the blow torch to light the make shift wick and explode the propane tank, was still holding his post like a true soldier. The silence was shattered by the sounds of big moving vehicles which sounded like construction trucks.

Somebody then sounded the alarm, "Yo, they're coming, they're coming!" After that you could hear the rallying calls of, "No justice, no peace!" and prisoners came flying outside from the blocks, with some type of weapon in their hands. Then the little brother and soldier with the blow torch took off running back towards us and dropped the torch on the walkway, as the troopers and trucks were moving close to our barricade.

A white inmate came rushing in out of nowhere, screaming, "Fuck that, light the tank!" and picked up the torch off of the walkway and ran towards the tank, followed by others with weapons, to initiate hand to hand combat with the troopers. Suddenly there was a "boom!" and the white inmate now holding the torch fell to the ground holding his stomach, and a black inmate and fellow comrade attempted to swoop in and grab the torch, but as soon as he bent down, there was another "boom", and he fell.

A truck bulldozed the make shift barricade and other prisoners came running up with weapons and towards the troopers. These dudes were serious about lighting the propane tank and serious about fighting with the state troopers. Then we heard more "Boom! Boom! Boom! Boom!" and saw bodies dropping on the ground left and right. "Retreat, retreat!" was yelled out to us and everybody ran to their blocks and cells. Joker came in behind me screaming, "They're shooking, they're shooking," imitating one of the Wayans brothers from the movie, "I'm Gonna Get You Sucker". As I began to look out of the window, he pulled me back away from it and said, "Stay out of the window, they got rifles now that shoot through brick walls." He looked at me seriously and then said, "No, for real."

Back in 1989, we had all heard of AK-47's and M16's, but few of us had actually seen them or knew the difference in rifles. Techs, Uzis, Glocks and Mac II's were common in the streets of Philadelphia, so I actually believed him. Then the irony was that what he was making up came to reality and there was a loud explosion on the block. We ran to the front of the cell and saw a white shirt with other officers climbing through a hole that they had blew into the wall in the back of the block, with rifles in their hands.

It seemed like they were mocking us and showing us how it's really done, because they had to use C-4 or a stick of dynamite to make that big of a hole as it did, instantly.

Joker then yelled to me, "Put your padlock on the bars so they can't come in the cell on us." But as we watched them pulling prisoners out of their cells—even ones who were waving white flags—and beating the shit out of them, my celly changed his mind. "Fuck that," he said. "Take that lock off of that door, because we know it's helicopters flying around out there filming so it we got to get our ass beat, let's get beat on camera."

That made all of the sense in the world and I started fidgeting with the lock, missing the combination as the guards with guns continued to sweep from cell to cell, snatching prisoners out and beating them. The dead corpse officer came running out of the side of the make shift yard where he laid with the sheet still on him, and to the troopers in the front of the block, who rushed him down the walkway past our window, and view to the walkway.

"That motherfucker wasn't dead," Joker said. "He was playing possum on us the whole time," he added. I replied, "I saw him myself and he wasn't breathing, moving or nothing. I swear I thought he was dead."

Joker's response to me was, "Fuck that, get that goddamn lock off that door."

"Snap!" was the sound when it finally opened, and not a minute too soon we were out of the cell and headed to the front of the block and looking back behind us, as the team of riot busters arrived at our cell.

At the front of the block was another team, but this time of all state troopers, with guns pointed at us. "Get down, get down on the ground and crawl out on your bellies if you want to come out alive," was the order that was barked to us. We formed two lines for the two doors that were open at the front of the block, got down on our stomachs and crawled out, two at a time. Once two prisoners got outside there were troopers on either side who secured us with plastic ties, patting us down, lifting us up and knocking or pulling any hats, *kufis*, etc., off of our heads, then spread rushing us to the yard, while partially dragging us.

We were all placed on both sides of the handball courts—the very last of the Camp Hill rioters. We were placed on our knees, facing the walls of the handball courts as the state troopers stood behind us, mostly, with a couple on either side of us. It was deadly silent where we were being held.

I looked around and saw that everybody else was being held in the yard, too, even the ones who turned themselves in the night before. They were mostly packed in on the other side of the yard. "That's what they get for being a bunch of cowards," I thought to myself. "They received a worse fate than us for giving up."

The troopers behind us must have unloaded their shotguns because they stood behind us with them to our heads and would pull the trigger one at a time, "Clack, clack," and we would jump, thinking that our brains were going to be blown out. After the second or third person jumped, I thought they were playing Russian Roulette because they would walk up behind you, pull the trigger, watch you jump, snigger and step back as the next of the gun men stepped up and did the same.

Finally and old head named Tone, from North Philly couldn't take it any more and snapped out, "Fuck that shit!" as he jumped to his feet, but still with his hands secured behind his back like the rest of us. "Fuck that, shoot me now, crackers!" he screamed. "Y'all going to kill me, then kill me now."

A couple more followed behind him and jumped up saying, "Fuck that, shoot me too." Then we all jumped up and screamed, "Shoot me, too!"

A white shirted state trooper, who was white, came over with another white shirted state trooper who was a female, and black like us. They walked up Tone and said, "Calm down." Tone said, "I can't take that shit. They're standing behind me pointing their shotguns at my head and pulling the trigger."

The white shirted trooper called to some of the troopers, and in a nice, calm voice said, "Take him over there." Some of the other prisoners said, "You take him, you got to take us too." The white shirted then barked, "Okay," and motioned for the others of his officers to escort those ones, too, as he led them all over to the ditches that were dug, and had them all thrown into it.

The rest of us sat right back down.

14

The cold rain began to fall again on the morning of October 27, 1989, as we sat there on our knees on the cement hand ball courts. Some of us were getting cramps or were losing circulation in different areas of their bodies, or were just aching from the beatings of the troopers and officers. If you complained or moved the wrong way you were beaten again out in the yard, then thrown in the holes or ditches they were digging, and we could smell the horse piss and shit from where we were at. We were the last inmates to be recaptured in the Camp Hill riot and the ones closest to the pits, for some reason.

The white shirted, white male trooper came back over and somebody from amongst us started pleading with him, "I can't feel my arms, man, and my knees are swelling up. You got to let me up for a minute and loosen these things." He was an older prisoner so the trooper came over and checked him out, then told his cronies to loosen up the plastic ties on him and let him get some circulation. Others started calling to him and pleading with him to loosen their binds, and some of them needed to use the bathroom, so he had all of us stand up and ordered the troopers to take our plastic ties from behind us and put them on in the front. They moved us all over to the grass by the fence and told us when we got there to face towards the fence and urinate if we had to.

The black female trooper walked over, being nosy, and saw and heard what he was doing and said, "No, you're not doing that. Don't loosen nothing up." The white shirt trooper just smiled and ignored her and kept doing what he was doing, so she ran off to a black heavy-set guy in a blue sweat suit and sneakers who was controlling the whole procedure. She brought him back over with her and started telling him the white, white shirt trooper was moving us over to the grass and adjusting our plastic ties.

The white, white shirt trooper and black fat guy in the blue jump suit both walked off to the side and started whispering between each other, as we watched. The black female trooper was watching too, and inmates from amongst us started verbally abusing her, saying, "Stinking bitch, you black like us, and going to stop the white man from helping us." and "I wish we would have caught your black jigga boo ass, we would have split your asshole in two, cracker lover." And so on, until finally the two returned and the blue jumpsuit guy took the black female trooper to the other side of the yard with him.

The white shirt trooper continued with what he was doing and we all were placed on the grass by the fence with our hands now secured in front of us. And what a big difference and relief that was. I even took a long held urine that I must have been holding on to all night, since we first came back out.

Only a few minutes had gone by from our bathroom break, in which we were initially told to face towards the fence, and now were being told to turn around and face in the opposite direction. At first, we were pleased with that and assumed that we had survived our torture period and the worst was over. How wrong again we all were.

We could look around and see the whole yard, and what everybody else in the yard and up to the walkway and leading into the compound were doing. We even had a view to the modular units and back walkway that led to the power house and administration building. This move was made intentionally, as we had to watch them line everybody else up that was in the yard and march them to the water fountains every hour, exactly. We could also see that Tone and his crew were still sitting in the holes that were dug in the yard, and not getting treated any better.

At the first hour of the water fountain privilege that the others were allowed to participate in, we watched as one by one, each inmate walked up to the water fountain and took deep, long sips of water. My mouth was all of a sudden instantly dry and sore, and I realized that it probably wasn't since we first came out, that I had actually drank any water. The only plus of that was I didn't have to urinate or defecate the rest of the day, like some of the others were having to do. But after the first hour of water drinking and every one of them having gone through the lines, it would start all over again like a revolving door, because it took that long to get to everybody.

Tone and his crew were placed back with us. Any of us who couldn't hold it and had to use the bathroom were led over to the holes dug in the yard, where Tone and company were pulled out of. The rest of the yard were taken to the inmate bathrooms that were originally made for us. As soon as anybody complained about it, or anything else, they were thrown in the muddy/shitty holes. So most of us just kept quiet.

15

The sun had come up by the noon hour and even though I was dying of thirst, it felt good because I was no longer cold and the damp prison browns were drying out. None of us had our coats on either, due to the troopers making us remove them before we crawled out of the blocks.

As evening came and the sun started to set, bag meals were passed out to us, which contained a baloney and cheese sandwich and a half a pint of milk. This time, though, we were the first to receive them, but had to eat them with our hands still secured in front of us with the plastic ties. It was the milk that was more soothing to me, so I passed my thin slice of baloney and two slices of cheese in between two thick slices of Camp Hill made bread, knowing that I'd still be thirsty and probably get heartburn eating it, and only having a half pint of milk to wash it down with. But I eagerly gulped down the milk, which felt refreshing, and like the best damn milk that I ever tasted in my life.

Within minutes after our feeding break was over and our now trash bags collected, about seven or eight PA DOC buses, better known as "blue gooses" to the prisoners, pulled up. There were only a few state prisons in Pennsylvania at that time, less than ten, so there was probably one sent from each prison. Now there are at least thirty prisons, of which each has at least two or three PA DOC buses to transfer prisoners back and forth around the state, at least on every Tuesday and Thursday.

We began to get excited again because we immediately thought Graterford was our destination. Graterford had an outside hole for prisoners called "Siberia" that had been recently shut down so we were hoping that they had opened it back up just for us, and this was the talk being whispered amongst us after seeing the blue gooses arrive. Anywhere in Graterford was good for us because we would still be at what we called "the party". Even if we had to land in "Siberia" for however long, that was acceptable to us and still the illusion that we all were under, as the majority of this bunch was from Philadelphia, both black and white, with very few Hispanics making up the rest.

We were eventually marched over to the buses. Our group of standouts filled the buses first, being placed in 32 inmates to each bus. Then the inmates from the rest of the yard were marched over to fill in the remainder, and the doors were shut and the buses pulled right out.

For us, those bus seats felt so comfortable and relaxing compared to what we had endured since day break. We started cheering and saying, "We're going to the party," and the guards driving and escorting the bus told us to shut up and remain quiet. But we were in full defiance now, being locked in amongst ourselves, with nobody standing by to whack us with billy clubs.

Verbal exchanges between us and them went on for about two hours, until we realized that we were nowhere near Graterford and should have been there by now. We then started asking the guards where they were taking us and received no response from them. That shut us up and we remained quiet for the next four or five hours, and even fell asleep.

Once we got near Three Rivers Stadium, some of the prisoners recognized it and let everybody else know. "We're in Pittsburgh, y'all, we're going to Western," was heard and I, along with everybody else, woke right up. "You mean we ended up all the way on the other side of the state, instead of Graterford," was heard from someone. We all felt deflated after that and fell silent again. Plus we knew we were about to exit the buses now and were again at the mercy of the billy clubs and all guards, no state troopers.

"Yeah, boys, they're waiting on y'all," came from one of the prison guards, at which "Fight the power!" was heard among our group members as an inspirational war cry and to reunite us.

16

As the group of blue gooses got close to the prison, the first thing we noticed was the giant wall surrounding it, which looked like something out of medieval times. It must have been in the early morning hours, maybe two or three a.m. We sat outside the prison and were taken in one bus at a time and unloaded, then marched straight to our cells on North block, which had been closed by the federal courts as condemned. We all knew that much, because it had been on the news and in the newspapers around the state months earlier. However, they had opened it back up, especially for us.

The cells where the North block was, sat in the back of the prison and were very small and damp. They had screws sticking up out of the floor from the desk and cabinet that had been removed from all of the cells, no telling how long ago, so you had to watch your step, specifically when getting out of your bunk. You could reach your arms out and touch each side of the walls. You also had to roll up your mattress on your bunk whenever you used the sink because it sat right over the end of the bunk closest to the back wall and your bunk or anything on top of it would get wet from the splash of water that shot back up and out from the sink.

Whenever you sat on the toilet your knees touched that end of the bunk as well. You could actually lounge on the toilet with your feet up on top of your bunk. And if you were Muslim, you would have to remove everything off of your bunk and make your prayers on top of the metal frame because there wasn't enough room anywhere else in the cell. We even had to place a cover over the toilets whenever we weren't using them—and have it weighted down with something—to keep any and everything from coming up out of them, supposedly from the river. Snakes, rats, insects had all been said to pop up out of those toilets on North block.

We even had bird's nests at the back of the block, which pigeons flew around freely, shitting up and down the tier. They would even come to your cell door if you fed them, and out on the tier if anything was dropped out there.

The good part was that we were at least given two sheets, a blanket, a bar of soap and a roll of toilet paper, and that was a first sense of comfort that we had thus far, and would get for the next few weeks. I guess the Pittsburgh officials were still trying to figure out what was what after the Graterford's mistake hours earlier.

It was much colder in Pittsburgh and the windows

which ran all the way up and down the block outside our cells were busted out. The river sat right there on the backside of North block where my cell happened to be and the gusts of wind that would come off of the river were biting.

Nobody slept. We all stood wrapped in our sheets and blankets at the door, calling out to each other to identify who was in what cell and on what tier, as North block was a total of five tiers high. We couldn't see up or down the tier, only what was directly in front of you. A wall on both sides of your doorway blocked off the view. Even the cell door and door way was small; we had to bend down to get out or back in the cells. But that problem didn't come for us for weeks after arriving there, as we were kept exclusively confined in the cells for that long.

We were fed breakfast on breakfast trays and received a hot lunch as well, and again for dinner, which was far better than the prisoners got that were still left out in the yard. The prison was now being searched and everything on the cell blocks removed and thrown away in the dumpsters that they had brought into the prison and set up on each side of the blocks. Everything was removed inside the cells as they went from block to block and the prisoners sat outside for days, almost a full week. Then they were placed back in the cells linked together in threes, so when one guy had to use the bathroom the other two had to stand right beside them, and if the guy in the middle had to defecate, when he wiped his ass, one of the other guys had to reach back there too. They had to use the sandwich bag or brown paper bag to wipe themselves with, as no toilet paper or soap was issued, as we had the luxury of, although nobody was receiving showers or a change of underclothes, not even us.

17

Back at SCI-Pittsburgh, a couple of white shirts, a captain and lieutenant, came around and told us to sign up for sick-call if we took any medication or had any issues. We were then told by them that the Governor had declared a state of emergency and now all of the prisons were operating under martial law, so we now had no rights, and that a total of about 500 prisoners had been brought to SCI-Pittsburgh and were now housed on North block. That was all we found out before they left.

We now got quiet and let the inmate closest to the middle of the tier yell over to the other side, as there was an opening platform between the tiers, and it was easier to converse with those on the other side. We then began finding out who was housed over there, and to my disappointment, most of my Southwest/West Philly homeboys were. Somehow in the joy of believing that we were headed to the "party", I had become separated from them. My boy Dino, Tokey, Rasul, Scarboy, Lil' Ronnie, Mah Dog, and even my celly, Joker, were all over there.

As night fell, the sound of screams and hollers could be heard coming from the other side of the tier. "Yo, y'all, what's going on over there?" our designated communicator called out. "The guards are running in cells beating us," the inmate on the other side called back.

We began shaking our gates and shouting obscenities to the guards doing the beatings, hoping to put some pressure on them to make them stop. We thought it worked after we didn't hear any more screams or yells, but every hour throughout the night they would sneak back, pop open a gate, and run in with disguises and beat them like clockwork. It was only happening on that side of North block which faced the inside, in the compound area. Our side faced the river, from which the tiers could clearly be seen at night from any of the river boats outside, or anybody who was in the back parking lot area. So we figured that the reason why they weren't coming around on our side was to not be seen by outsiders. There weren't any cameras recording in any of the prisons in the State of Pennsylvania back then, either.

As a precaution, we tied our sheets, socks and/or browns we wore from our cell doors to our bunks so that the hit squad of officers couldn't just run in on us, and basically stayed awake for the next three days. On the third day exhaustion hit us and we all fell asleep during the day but were again by nightfall. That became our normal schedule: sleep during the day, and be up and ready at night.

Eventually, the state of emergency was called off by the governor and SCI-Pittsburgh was off lock down. The prison guards then allowed inmate workers from their prison quarantine which housed their parole violators and new arrivals waiting to be classified then shipped to another prison inside the PA DOC. By them, we were able to get the word out to the Muslim and inmate population about the hit squad of guards during the night. Muslims, freedom fighters and revolutionaries from the general population then all got together and marched over to North block and demanded that the hit squad and inmate beatings during the night be stopped, and even threatened retaliation for them if they continued.

The hit squad and beatings stopped that same night. However, they came up with another form of retaliation by ordering us not to talk on the gate at night and issuing multiple misconduct reports arbitrarily. We couldn't be taken to their hole, or even out of our cells, for any reason but for those who had a minimum date coming up or were a parole violator, which most of our bunch were, the reports ended up catching up to you and we received a hit from the parole board of extra months added on. They even had a black female officer patrol the tiers at night and we were issued reports for allegedly threatening her, using obscene or abusive language to her, or disobeying a direct order. The direct order disobeyed was for something they made up, that they called "reckless eyeballing" and of course we were found guilty of every charge and every report, so basically, we couldn't even look at her without being penalized.

As weeks went by and the Thanksgiving holiday came around we were given toothpaste and toothbrushes and all permitted a shower, but the towels given to us by the guards were so small that you couldn't wrap them around you unless you had a very small waist. After all we endured in the yard at Camp Hill and the three weeks at SCI-Pittsburgh, and this being the only chance we were given to come out of our cells or shower, most of us, including myself, came out handcuffed in front with only a towel in our hands, naked. We were let out in groups of three and were walked down the tier and steps to the back showers. We respected each other's privacy being nude, and as the showers were all filled and the gate locked, were then given a, five minute exactly, shower: one minute to get wet, two minutes to lather up and two minutes to rinse off—probably less, as an officer stood by timing each one with his wrist watch and barking out each cycle. Then the showers were immediately turned off and we were marched back to our cells, some still with lather in their hair or on their bodies, and upset.

By the time the Christmas season of 1989 had come around, we were allowed to purchase commissary orders and take showers three times a week, with underwear and towels. The holiday season even brought down the tension from the SCI-Pittsburgh officers who were now patrolling the tiers and talking trash to us, such as, "You young niggas from Philadelphia ain't tough. Y'all screamed, cried and hollered all night long when we were beating y'all ass. But Jeff Mims now, we beat and beat that nigga all night long and he didn't scream, holler or flinch, not one damn time." Then added, "Shi-i-it, that's the toughest damn nigga from Philly we ever saw." Which we even had to laugh at ourselves, especially remembering those nights back then: how inmates, grown men, were crying, hollering and screaming, even ones on our side of the tier who weren't getting beaten. And Jeff Mims was truly a legend as a tough ass old head from Philadelphia. We might have even been letting out some of the joy and tension that those days were now over for us. They even started allowing us to make one phone call a week to our family and loved ones.

18

The New Year of 1990 ushered in and most of our Camp Hill bunch were now transferred temporarily to the federal bureau of prisons for six months and others back to Camp Hill to be formally charged for their alleged parts of the riots, mostly being accused and pointed out by other inmates.

One of most notorious finger pointers and accusers was an inmate called Big Ron from north Philadelphia. Big Ron was a large, muscular, street and prison supposedly tough guy, who was big and athletic with a bald head and deep baritone voice. So it came as a surprise to us that he would be snitching on inmates, about a prison riot especially.

Months later, after landing at SCI-Huntington and seeing him down in the gym playing basketball for the prison's varsity team, and having inmates in the bleachers boo and berate him about being a finger pointer to even truly innocent inmates, Big Ron got tough again now and walked over to those inmates and said, "Fuck it, that's right, I did it," then added, "They told me if I did it I'd be guaranteed to make parole on my minimum and I want to go home, so now."

What his dumb ass didn't know was that unless they were charging him for something, he was going to get paroled anyway. The PA parole board was letting inmates go home more easily back then so he really didn't get anything for his assistance with PA DOC, not even a furlough. But he did get to make his parole and what he did get as well was his brains blown right out as soon as he got there. I don't know if it was because of his part in the finger pointing and accusing inmates of the Camp Hill riot, but I'm just saying, what a hell of a coincidence and it bought joy and was news all over the PA prison system.

No Justice, No Peace…No Justice, No Peace…!

19

Once the SCI-Camp Hill infamous group of about 500 was withered down to about 30 or 40 now housed on the once condemned North block at SCI-Pittsburgh, we were now allowed two hours, sometimes more, recreation time in the North block yard. They would issue us used coats for the yard period but collect them back once our yard period was over. It was dead cold and the hale was treacherous but we would all go out together and would all be bunched up together talking and joking the whole time, feet and toes frozen, ears and hands as well but we were there.

The officers were well aware of the camaraderie that we had amongst us, so they would just leave us locked out in the yard together without standing out there with us or even watching from a post somewhere. We definitely didn't have any anger issues or beefs within by now regardless of what race, religious belief, sexual preference or location you were from or represented. By now we had all pulled together and supported each other in any way that we could in order to help each other get through it. Those few months now felt like we had known each other for years and were one big family. We'd come out, smoke, joke, and pass around commissary items, then go back in. And if one inmate amongst had a problem with an officer we all did, but by that time they had pulled back and eased up on us. So there were never any issues or problems during our yard recreation periods except the damn cold.

We eventually got down to the last ten to twelve inmates and we were given a choice to either take prison browns and go out to their general population on South block, or prison blues and stay in quarantine on North block and await a transfer to another PA state prison. I chose blues because I wanted the hell out of cold ass Pittsburgh, where snowflakes had fallen even in April.

August came around and I was told to pack up because I was being transferred out, finally. When I went down and had my property packed to be shipped with me, the sergeant who was packing me up and had been working on North block our whole time there said to me, "You know, I haven't said a word to you the whole time you've been here but I sort of like you even though you're a big mouth, so I'm leaving you with this little advice. You're going to SCI-Huntington, so when you get there make sure you be very careful about what you say to them officers on your way in there, especially with that big box haircut that you've got," then added after pausing, "I'm serious, be careful." I didn't know what he meant exactly, although I had already hear stories of how racist Huntington was, and prepared myself for it.

As the blue goose arrived at SCI-Huntington between 1:30 and 2:00 p.m. we were greeted by a kangaroo line of officers, both from the 6 to 2 shift and the 2 to 10 shift. Two lines of officers with huge billy clubs stood on both sides as we were let down out of the back of the bus and had to walk through it. The officers shouted, "You's at Huntington now boys," and other things to intimidate us or disrespect us and to initiate a response, at which they would then use those billy clubs on us. And it became even clearer what the sergeant back at Pittsburgh had already known and was trying to warn me of.

I walked through the middle of this man made tunnel that led straight to B block, which was the hole and death row, to wait in a room to be seen and screened by the inmate review committee to see if they'd place you in their general population or their hole. I looked at the first cell right there by the officer's desk and it was none other than Bro. Kareem, the Camp Hill FOI inmate minister and second leader of October 25th and leader on October, 26, 1989.

He looked worn and beat up and in need of a haircut and shave, which he probably hadn't had since October, 1989. It was now August, 1990, and he looked much older, as if he had aged by years and not only months. It caught me off guard and I didn't know what to say or do, as we looked at each other and I was put in the shower room with the others to be seen and called one at a time by IRC to find out our fate. The IRC asked questions about my misconducts but their only real concern was if I was involved in the Camp Hill riot, and of course I answered them, "No!"

I was released to general population and met up with others I had known and the Muslims in the community there, and wasted no time mentioning Bro. Kareem being back in the hole. I was then told that our once-Muslim Amir and leader on the first night of the Camp Hill riot was back there in the hole too, along with all of the Muslims who had retaliated and rioted at Huntington, from which our inspiration had come. This was probably the main reason for the sergeant's warning when he had packed me up.

Years later on a second sentence I was now doing in 2012, I ran into Bro. Kareem in the big yard at SCI-Dallas and we embraced and conversed among ourselves for hours. He told me how they beat and treated him after the riot and the years that he spent in the hole, and he had just spent another five years in the hole there under a false pretense of a bogus investigation that he was trying to plan a riot there, before making it back into general population.

I had already come across Ameen in general population back in the 1990's at SCI-Huntington, once he was released from the hole and went on to become the Amir of the Sunni Muslim community there, which I informed Bro. Kareem of. That was the last meeting and conversation we had while I was at SCI-Dallas with Bro.

Kareem who was still an FOI but seemed more of a loner and as if he had issues going on, not with the administration but instead within himself. No respect was lost though, as again we were forever forged together as comrades and soldiers at arms at the 1989 Camp Hill Riot.

20

The year was now 2005 and I was being held in PICC, a county prison on State Rd. in Philadelphia. I had been arrested for an arsenal of weapons: three AK-47's, and AR-15 assault rifle, a sawed-off shotgun, numerous handguns and two Kevlar bullet proof vests, and was awaiting to be released on bail. I was awakened out of my bunk by a loud mouth new arrival on the block and got up to see who he was and when I looked out of my cell door, I had to look twice at the familiar face at the desk. "Dino!" I yelled out of my door, and ran out to greet him.

He was now older and heavier, wilder and battle scarred, but still my old buddy Dino. I hadn't seen him since 1993 at the bar on 60th and Delancy in his neighborhood, with his sidekick Tokey. He told me that right after that last meeting, Tokey had gone down to Virginia and tried to rob a bank, got caught and received a 25 year sentence. He had heard about my case in a southwest Philly newspaper and said to me, "They said you had enough artillery in that house to start a riot." He then added, "What the hell was you doing boy, getting Camp Hill flashbacks?" And we laughed hardy like old times.

I immediately moved him in my cell and put up with his now crazy ass for days. And just like old times he had been sent there from the Philadelphia Detention Center for stabbing another inmate.

"Why did you stab him Dino?" I asked him. "Because he was a damn rat!" he answered back. I then stated to him, "I got a serious damn question for you, oh boy, and I want a serious damn answer out of you."

"Okay," he said, and added, "But don't shoot!"

"How many damn people did you stab in the Camp Hill riot? And don't lie to me either, motherfucker." I asked and said. "No damn body," was his quick response and we both busted out laughing again. We both ended up being bailed out and back on the streets together.

It was now the summer of 2006, and while riding down 60th street near the bar on Delancy, I again noticed the familiar face of Dino, so I pulled over and parked.

We stood outside the bar talking about old times and how old we were now getting. He asked me if I remembered Ole Joe from West Philly, who suffered a blood clot in his head after being beaten by the prison guards. I said, "Yeah, how could I ever forget him and the white prison guard." He then said, "He still has brain damage."

"Damn, that's fucked up," I said.

"He's right in the bar now with a white girl he married," Dino said. "You want to see him?"

"Yeah, man, come on," I said and walked towards to bar. When I walked in I immediately noticed him sitting up at the back bar with a white female next to him. I went up and spoke to him and asked him if he remembered me, which he did, and he introduced me to his wife. He then invited me and Dino to his van with him and his wife to talk, so we all then headed outside and followed Joe.

When we arrived at the van it looked old and raggedy and like they were living inside of it together so I let Dino, Joe and his wife get inside while I stood on the outside. Joe then started talking and pulled out a bag of cocaine and a straw and began snorting from it. He passed the bag and straw my way and I declined. He offered Dino some, who eagerly snorted from it then passed it to the white girl and wife. They snorted and we conversed for a little while and then I excused myself. My excuse was I had to go pick up my wifey.

That was the last I saw of Joy or my boy Dino to this day. As we pass by in life now—has-beens and washed up—I can't help but pat myself on the back and beat my chest, knowing that we really made history and are forever forged and bonded together as comrades of the struggle. See us now... oh well... but had you seen us back on those two dates, October 25 and 26, 1989 at SCI-Camp Hill PA, then you just might understand why, and what I'm talking about, booouy! Believe that!!!

ABOUT THE AUTHOR

Derrick Gibson is a former street hustler, drug dealer, optician, and paralegal.

He is presently the author of three novels. Derrick —born and raised in the mean streets of Philadelphia, Pennsylvania—was educated in the Philadelphia school system, then to the school of hard knocks: Glen Mills Reform School, Philadelphia County Prison, Philadelphia Department of Corrections, and eventually the Federal Bureau of Prisons before calling it quits.

Derrick gravitated to his penmanship producing his first book *Before Orange was the New Black,* and is also producing two other novels, *6-O-Kings Chesseing* and *6-O-Kings Brass Brothers.*

www.ingramcontent.com/pod-product-compliance
Lightning Source LLC
LaVergne TN
LVHW051507070426
835507LV00022B/2966